LONDON

LONDON

IAIN THOMSON

GRAMERCY BOOKS
NEW YORK

This 2000 edition is published by Gramercy Books™,
a division of Random House Value Publishing, Inc.,
280 Park Avenue, New York, NY 10017.
by arrangement with PRC Publishing Ltd.
Kiln House, 210 New Kings Road, London SW6 4NZ

Gramercy Books™ and design are registered trademarks of
Random House Value Publishing, Inc.
Random House
New York • Toronto • London • Sydney • Auckland
http://www.randomhouse.com/

Printed and bound in China
A CIP catalogue record for this book is available from the Library of Congress.

ISBN 0-517-16174-5

8 7 6 5 4 3 2 1

ACKNOWLEDGMENTS
The publisher wishes to thank Pictor for supplying all the photography for this book,
including the photographs on the front and back jacket, with the following exceptions:
Dave Gadd/Allstar for pages 9, 13, 25, 38, 66 and 115;
Duncan Willetts/Allstar for pages 14, 30, 51 and 60;
© Reuters Newmedia Inc/CORBIS for page 26;
© Philippa Lewis; Edifice/CORBIS for pages 24-25;
© Julia Waterlow; Eye Ubiquitous/CORBIS for pages 44-45;
© London Aerial Photo Library/CORBIS for pages 56-57 and 80-81;
© WildCountry/CORBIS for pages 62-63;
© Cordaiy Photo Library Ltd./CORBIS for pages 68-69;
Paul McFegan/Allstar for page 71;
© Jeremy Horner/CORBIS for pages 76-77;
© Rupert Horrox/CORBIS for pages 84-85;
© John Heseltine/CORBIS for pages 92-93;
© Adam Woolfitt/CORBIS for pages 96-97;
Allstar for page 107;
© Bob Krist/CORBIS for pages 108-109;
© Jonathan Blair/CORBIS for pages 112-113;
© Geoffrey Taunton; Cordaiy Photo Library Ltd./CORBIS for pages 116-117.

Front jacket:

Westminster Bridge & Palace of Westminster

A view of the Houses of Parliament and the 19th century Westminster Bridge from the south bank of the Thames.

Page 2

The Tower of London and Tower Bridge

Aerial view over the City of London looking towards the south-east.

Back jacket:

Regent Street

Regent Street, one of the finest shopping streets in the world, was laid out by the great architect John Nash on the orders of George IV.

CONTENTS

INTRODUCTION

London, the capital of England, chief city of the Commonwealth of Nations, and largest city of the United Kingdom, is located in south-east England at the head of the Thames estuary to the west of its mouth on the North Sea. London is one of the world's foremost financial, commercial, industrial, and cultural centers, as well as being one of its greatest ports. The city is made up of 32 boroughs and the Corporation of London—the City—each with its own local government. The City, with an area of one square mile, is the historical and commercial core of London, has its own constitution, and elects the lord mayor.

The origin of the name of London's river is unknown but Julius Caesar spoke of the "Tamesis." Until the latter part of the 19th century the river was wide and dirty, being the main receptacle of the city's waste. The muddy banks smelled of refuse and were littered with debris and apart from Southwark, at the south end of London Bridge, much of the south bank was not even built over. London Bridge was the only crossing until 1750 when a second bridge was built at Westminster. Although the number of bridges rapidly increased, the southern banks of the Thames remained largely insignificant. Several times in the 16th and 17th centuries, when it froze over, the river was the setting for huge fairs where oxen were roasted on the thick ice. Even into Victorian times the Thames still froze hard enough to allow "Frost Fairs" to be held on its surface. The Thames in London is tidal and the city has been a port for seagoing vessels since the Roman period. The main port has now moved much further downstream from the old Pool of London and the river is currently one of the cleanest city rivers in the world.

Little is known of the city prior to Queen Boudicca's revolt against the Romans in AD 61 but it has been established that the first settlement, the Roman Londinium, was founded in AD 43 on a terrace near the north bank of the River Thames after Aulus Plautius, the commander of the Roman invasion force, was obliged to build a bridge there. At first the crossing was only of military use to the Romans but the bridge became a focal point and the settlement soon became an important trading post. During the 1st century AD it became

Left:
Harrods
The frontage of Harrods, the largest department store in Europe. The legend of Harrods is that there is nothing that cannot be purchased there.

a town of considerable importance, although not an administrative center. The Roman town occupied roughly the same area as the "square mile" of the City today. The Romans built their town here as it was the furthest point up the Thames that ships could easily reach on the tide, and the geological conditions meant the river could be bridged. The original London Bridge was probably built between AD 100 and AD 400. The Romans were temporarily removed when Queen Boudicca sacked their town in AD 60, but they returned and strengthened their settlement with a wall about two miles in perimeter, 20 feet high, and nine feet thick and from this time London became the administrative center of Roman Britain. Remains of this wall can be seen today in Coopers Row where Roman coins are still being found.

The Roman legions eventually withdrew in the 5th century and the importance of the city's site declined. Celts, Saxons, and Danes contested the area, but it was not until 886 that London emerged as an important town under King Alfred when it gradually reasserted itself to become a prosperous trade center. By 1017 the Danish King Canute (995–1035) ruled, and under him Danish traders were allowed to settle in London. Under his successor, Edward the Confessor (c. 1002–66), who was Norman by descent, French influence came to the town.

London was now the largest, most important and prosperous city in the land but it was not yet the capital. Only after Edward restored the ancient monastery at Westminster and his successor, Harold (c. 1022–66), was crowned there could London truly claim to be the capital of England. It was really a capital with two centers—the City, ruled by merchants and the guilds, and Westminster, where the monarch had his palace. In 1066 when the Normans invaded Britain, William the Conqueror (c. 1028–87) granted London its charter and also made the city his capital. The original Roman wall, built some 1,000 years earlier, was still large enough to contain William's city and he set about building a great castle —the Tower of London—to create a center for defense and a citadel to overawe the populace.

Under the Normans and Plantagenets London became self-governing and grew commercially and politically. By the 14th century it had become the political capital of England, the largest city, and chief port. When the Tudor Henry VIII (1491–1547) came to the throne in 1509, London's population was about 50,000 but by the end of the century it had grown to about 200,000. New palaces were built to replace the Tower as the royal residence, notably Westminster, Whitehall, and St. James's, and the city reached a new level of pre-eminence during the reign of Queen Elizabeth I (1558–1603) when it became the center of England's Renaissance. The opening of the Royal Exchange in 1566 heralded the growth of the city in world importance—in the years that followed, William Shakespeare's (1564–1616) plays were first performed in the Globe Theatre, book publishing began, and London became the center of England's newly emerging foreign trade.

Above:

Petticoat Lane Market

The street market acquired the name Petticoat Lane during the
17th century because of the number of old clothes dealers
who congregated here.

James I (1566–1625) bestowed on London two great achievements: the architecture of Inigo Jones (1573–1652) and Middleton's New River Project. London's growing population badly needed new sources of fresh water, and Hugh Middleton's (1560–1631) great engineering venture to bring fresh water to London from Hertfordshire would have failed but for James's financial backing. Inigo Jones, undoubtedly the greatest architect of his day, was appointed Surveyor of the Royal Buildings, and his influence on building designs in the capital was enormous. With the Restoration of the monarchy and King Charles II's (1630–85) return from exile in 1660, the repressive dictatorship of the Commonwealth ended. Theaters were allowed to reopen and restrictions on building were eased allowing developers to build new houses in the rapidly-expanding and increasingly fashionable West End.

By the early 17th century London was a busy, crowded capital city of narrow and twisting streets. In 1665, the Great Plague swept the city and nearly 70,000 Londoners succumbed to the disease. Within a year this dreadful epidemic was followed by the Great Fire of 1666, which started when a baker's oven overheated in Pudding Lane on September 2, 1666. Because most of the buildings in the city were made of wood the conflagration quickly spread, and 13,000 houses were destroyed. Remarkably, only four people were killed. Only Staple Inn in Holborn survives today as an example of what the buildings in London looked like at that time. Immediately after the fire the Rebuilding Act of 1667 was passed decreeing that all new buildings had to be

Above:

Sir William Chambers's Chinese Pagoda

Sir William Chambers's Chinese Pagoda in Kew Gardens stands ten stories
(163 feet high). It was inspired by a visit to China in the architect's youth.

built in stone or brick! So by the late 17th century an entirely new city had
arisen out of the ashes and bore little resemblance to the quaint wooden
dwellings of old London. The rebuilding was distinguished by the work of the
architect Sir Christopher Wren (1632–1723), notably in St. Paul's Cathedral
(built on the site of the old 7th century cathedral) and over 50 city churches of
which more than 20 survive today.

   In the 18th century the city again began to grow, and the walls and gates of
the city, among the last vestiges of the medieval town, were demolished in the
1760s. With the building of elegant housing to the west and north-west of the
old city London became the focus, not only of politics, but of literary and artis-
tic society. The population started to grow rapidly and developers like the
Grosvenor family began to build in Mayfair and St. James. The main archi-
tectural innovations of this period were "the square" and building in
fashionable terraces. The royal parks, once royal hunting grounds and estates,

were gradually opened to the public and modern London is noted for its abundance of these park spaces—particularly St. James's Park, Green Park, Hyde Park, Regent's Park, and Kensington Gardens. For many Londoners the 18th century was a time of great opportunity, increasing wealth, and tremendous enjoyment.

London grew enormously in the 19th century, acquiring great prestige in the Victorian era as the capital of the British Empire. Urban development continued, with industrial suburbs spreading to the north-east and east of the city and the docks and dock-related industries spreading downriver. The docks were originally located near London Bridge in the city center, but in recent years these inner docks have been replaced by larger and more modern facilities to the east of the capital. The arrival of the railway created another wave of development in the late 1800s and large railway stations were built all round the edge of the main town. London was the first great city to be served by a railway network radiating nationwide and great Victorian termini ring the city center. To the north of Oxford Street, along the Marylebone, Euston, Pentonville, and City roads, the major railroad companies located the stations of Paddington, Marylebone, Euston, St. Pancras, King's Cross and Liverpool Street. The original Midland Grand Hotel, designed by George Gilbert Scott (1811–78) in 1865, forms the amazing facade of St. Pancras station. With its high pinnacles, towers, and gables it looks more like a Gothic castle than a railway station. It was closed as a hotel in the 1930s and is now used as offices though there is talk of redeveloping it as a luxury hotel.

In 1890 the world's first electric underground railroad was built and, during this Victorian era, straight, elegant streets were constructed through the congested inner city. Open spaces, such as Trafalgar Square, were also created. The 19th century was a period of reform and saw the establishment of municipal services: in 1829, Sir Robert Peel (1788–1850) established the Metropolitan Police Force with its world-famous "bobbies" named after him. Many suburbs were incorporated into Greater London, all the bridges in the city were rebuilt in stone, and the streets were newly illuminated, first with gas and later with electricity.

As a result of the blitz in World War II the 1950s saw war-damaged London being rebuilt again and, as in the reconstruction after the great fire in 1666, the character and the skyline of the city began changing. What was probably the most notable change came in the 1960s with the 30-story Museum Radio Tower of the General Post Office building (built in 1965) dominating the West End. Today the London skyline is studded with tower blocks and a number of business skyscrapers rather than spires and church towers. Development continued in the 1980s and 1990s with some high-rise buildings, particularly in the finacial center, but London has remained more immune to this form of development than most cities. In the shadow of the tower blocks and skyscrapers, the spires and church towers still exist. In the new millennium London is a modern city but still retains architecture from the last thousand years.

One of London's oldest landmarks, the Tower of London, is arguably the most venerable building in the city; the White Tower, in the center of the present complex, is the oldest and most impressive building dating from the period of William the Conqueror. He began building the Tower soon after the Battle of Hastings in 1066, and successive monarchs added to it until Edward I (1239–1307) completed the outer wall in the late 13th century. In 1483 the two princes, the young Edward V (1470–83) and his brother Richard (1473–83), were murdered in the Garden Tower, which was thereafter known as the "Bloody Tower." The Tower of London became the symbol of ultimate power and has served as a royal residence and a state prison, in which capacity it has seen many famous prisoners and executions; a stone in the pavement outside the Tower marks the principal execution site of traitors imprisoned there. Beheadings were carried out there for nearly 360 years, from Sir Simon de Burley, tutor to Richard II (1367–1400), in 1388 to Jacobite Lord Lovat in 1747. Although a great number of prisoners had been detained in the Tower since its construction, it was not until the Reformation brought Henry VIII's victims there that harsh treatment of prisoners became the norm. The Tower's most famous prisoner was probably Sir Walter Raleigh (c. 1552–1618), who lived fairly comfortably for 13 years in the upper floors of the Bloody Tower. The last prisoner held in the Tower was Rudolf Hess (1894–1987) during World War II; he was held for four days in the Lieutenant's Lodgings where, nearly 350 years earlier, Guy Fawkes and his accomplices were interrogated.

James I was the last monarch to use the Tower as a palace. He was interested in the royal menagerie and animal fights were regularly staged there until a small child was killed by a bear in 1609. In its time the Tower has housed the royal armories, the mint, the royal observatory, and the public records. Today the Tower is the home of the crown jewels and the world-famous "Beefeaters," the Yeomen of the Guard.

Adjacent to the historical Tower of London the famous and distinctive Victorian structure, Tower Bridge, spans the Thames. Tower Bridge is one of the most instantly recognizable bridges in the world and until November 1991, when the Queen Elizabeth Bridge at Dartford was opened, it was the only span across the Thames below London Bridge. Last century, London Bridge was the only practical way over the Thames and the horse-drawn carriages would sometimes queue for hours to cross. So, in 1876, it was decided to build a new bridge. To allow the large-masted ships of the day to sail up the Thames the bridge had to offer 140 feet clearance but the approaches couldn't be too steep as horse-drawn carriages had to cross. To solve these problems a raising bridge was designed. The bridge was built at a cost of £1,184 000, and ten lives, and was opened on June 30, 1894, by the Prince and Princess of Wales. It was a masterpiece of its time and such is its importance today that it is one

Above:

"Beefeaters"

The Yeoman Warders of the Tower of London and the Queen's Bodyguard of the
Yeomen of the Guard both wear Tudor uniform. The body of warders was founded
by Edward VI; the bodyguard—the oldest in the world—in 1485 by Henry VII.

of the few bridges in the world to have a museum dedicated to it and has
become a symbol of London.

To the west of Tower Bridge lies the City—the heart of London and its
financial district. The City is noted for its exchange and commodity markets,
insurance and banking functions, and a host of specialized services. In popular
and traditional usage, the term "City of London," or "the City," is applied only
to a small area that was the original settlement (Londinium) and is now part of
the business and financial district of the capital and is home to many historical
landmarks. In the heart of the city stands the Guildhall, dating from 1411, when
the livery companies raised money for its construction. The livery companies
date back to the time of King John (1167–1216) when, in 1215, he signed a
charter which gave the citizens of the City of London (the area enclosed by the
old Roman Wall) the right to elect their own mayor. These companies, or
guilds, evolved as friendly societies for members of a particular trade or craft
and, as they became more influential, leading members took to wearing distinctive costumes, or liveries, many of which are still worn during special
ceremonies. The Great Hall of the Guildhall is used for the Lord Mayor's
Banquet and is decorated with the colorful shields of the livery companies.

Running south from Holborn Viaduct, which was completed in 1869 to
bridge the Fleet river valley, is Old Bailey—the street which gives its name
to the Central Criminal Court. The notorious Newgate Prison, the scene of

Above:

Eros

Above the Shaftesbury Memorial Fountain in Piccadilly Circus is the first London statue cast in aluminum. Eros has spent two long periods away from home: in 1922–31 the memorial moved to Embankment Gardens while Piccadilly Circus tube station was built; during World War II it was stored at Egham.

public executions until 1868, stood on this site until it was demolished in 1902 and replaced by the court. Most of the major trials of the 20th century have been heard here, and the public may view the proceedings in Number One Court by queueing for a seat in the Visitors' Gallery. The southern end of Old Bailey joins Ludgate Hill, named after the Lud Gate which, tradition says, was built by King Lud in 66BC.

At the top of Ludgate Hill stands St. Paul's Cathedral, the fifth cathedral to be built on the site. The present St. Paul's was designed by Sir Christopher Wren after the Great Fire of 1666 had all but destroyed the previous building. The foundation stone was laid in 1675 and the final stone was laid by Wren's son in 1710, only 35 years after the work had begun—a considerable achievement for such a vast undertaking at a time when every stone was cut and put into position by hand. The beautiful, great central dome which Wren envisaged instead of the usual tall steeple or spire, although posing him considerable structural problems, proved to be a supreme example of his genius, and is today one of London's most recognizable landmarks. The great dome, which rises to 365 feet above ground level and is 112 feet in diameter, rises above the center of the nave. Around its interior is the famous Whispering Gallery, where a message whispered into the wall on one side can be clearly heard 112 feet away on the other side. Sir Christopher Wren is buried in the crypt of the cathedral, as are Lord Nelson and the Duke of Wellington. Despite its seeming vulnerability, St. Paul's remained remarkably unscathed during the Luftwaffe's fierce incendiary bomb attacks in the vicinity during World War II.

To the east of St. Paul's, along Cheapside, stands the "Old Lady of Threadneedle Street"—the Bank of England. This magnificent neo-classical building, surrounded by a windowless wall, was greatly reconstructed by the end of the 18th century. The vaults of the Bank traditionally house the nation's gold reserves, and the internal security system is, therefore, of the highest order. After the Bank was attacked by looters in 1780 the Bank Piquet was instituted, whereby a detachment of Guards marched to the building each afternoon and remained on watch throughout the night. This ceremony continued until an electronic security system was installed in 1973. South-west of the Bank stands the Mansion House, official residence of the Lord Mayor of London during his term of office. The foundation stone was laid in 1739, but few of the original fittings survived Victorian alterations. There was a general restoration of the whole structure during the 1930s, refurnishing it to its original style. Many historical artifacts are kept in the building including the 15th century mayoral Chain of Office, the 17th century Sword of State, and the 18th century Great Mace.

East of the City the old "East End" of London, with its cockneys and commercial docks, has largely disappeared. Whitechapel was, of course, the scene of the infamous Jack the Ripper murders in 1888 and Stepney's Limehouse area, which was London's original Chinatown, is now an upper-class residential area. The Port of London, once the main artery for the import of most goods into Britain, has declined due to the rise of the airport, the container ship, and the Channel Tunnel. The area has now been reclaimed and Dockland has experienced a vast wave of redevelopment, breathing new vitality into the area with residential conversions of warehouses and the building of new business facilities, like the Canary Wharf complex on the Isle of Dogs. The origin of the name of this peninsula, created by the great bend in the Thames opposite Greenwich, is thought to have derived from the royal kennels established there under Charles II.

Opposite the Isle of Dogs—and connected by a Victorian foot tunnel—stands Greenwich, with all its seafaring connections such as the Royal Naval College, the *Cutty Sark*, the National Maritime Museum, and the original Royal Observatory with the Greenwich Meridian. Traditional attractions there include many buildings designed by well-known English architects, including the Royal Naval College, the National Maritime Museum, and the

Old Royal Observatory situated in Greenwich Park, built by Sir Christopher Wren for King Charles II. Charles II founded the Royal Observatory in 1675 for the assistance of navigation but it was transferred in the early 1950s to Sussex and the buildings became part of the National Maritime Museum. At the Observatory, visitors can stand astride the Greenwich Meridian at longitude zero with one foot in the western hemisphere and the other in the eastern. Queen's House, initially built to designs by Inigo Jones for Anne of Denmark and noted as the first Palladian-style villa in England, formed the focal point of the Royal Naval Hospital, a group of buildings designed by Wren and Webb in the late 17th and early 18th centuries. In 1873 the hospital became the Royal Naval College. In 1954 the *Cutty Sark*, the last and most famous of the old tea clippers, was brought to dry dock in Greenwich and today Sir Francis Chichester's yacht *Gypsy Moth IV* lies nearby. Greenwich also played host to Britain's Millennium celebrations in the year 2000. It is anticipated that many millions of visitors from all over the world will visit the exhibition site, comprising, among other attractions, the Millennium Dome—the largest structure in the world. Within the dome, 12 zones, each containing a different theme, fan out from a central piazza.

Back up the Thames, past Tower Bridge and the Tower of London to where the river bends about 90 degrees to the south, lies the City of Westminster which officially covers almost all the area known as London's "West End." The name Westminster, however, more usually refers to the area immediately around the Houses of Parliament and Westminster Abbey. It began its development before the Norman Conquest, when Edward the Confessor built his palace there and established Westminster Abbey. Edward was determined to the abbey should see the coronation of English kings: his successor, Harold, was the first, crowned there the week after Edward's death in 1065; since then, every English sovereign has been crowned in the abbey, with the exceptions of Edward V and Edward VIII (1894–1972) who were never crowned. The abbey is a splendid example of English Gothic architecture and was rebuilt by Henry III (1207–72) in 1245 then altered and added to through the succeeding centuries. The abbey is crowded with tombs and monuments to royalty, statesmen, soldiers, poets, artists, and all manner of historical figures. Since a monument to Chaucer was erected in 1556 it has been the final accolade for a poet to be commemorated in what is now known as "Poet's Corner," although few of them are actually buried within the precincts of the abbey. One of the most visited tombs is that of the "Unknown Soldier," whose body was brought home from France after World War I. The abbey has also long been the setting of royal weddings and somber state occasions—such as the recent funeral of the tragic Diana, Princess of Wales.

Across the road from the abbey stands the Palace of Westminster built between 1840 and 1860 to replace the old palace. A fire in 1834 destroyed most of the medieval palace, in various buildings of which Parliament had met since

Above:

The Royal Observatory, Greenwich

The observatory was set up in the reign of Charles II, who provided building
materials but reneged on his agreement to buy instruments! The first Astronomer
Royal, John Flamsteed, laid the foundation stone and Sir Christopher Wren
designed the building.

the early 16th century. Sir Charles Barry's (1795–1860) great Perpendicular
Gothic replacement provided a building worthy of being the Houses of
Parliament, the nerve center of the nation's law-making and administration.
Barry's structure stood intact for nearly a century, but in May 1941 the House
of Commons was reduced to rubble by the Luftwaffe. It was rebuilt in the tradition of the old chamber and was completed in 1950. At the south of the
building is the lofty Victoria Tower (336 feet) and at the north end is the slight-
ly smaller, but much more famous Clock Tower (316 feet) known to all as Big
Ben. The name more accurately refers to the mighty 13.5 ton bell which strikes
the hours with its world-famous chime.

To the south of Victoria Street, which runs westward from Parliament
Square, stands Westminster Cathedral. This Roman Catholic cathedral is of an
early Christian Byzantine style of architecture and has the widest nave in
England. The interior is ornamented with more than 100 different kinds of
marble quarried worldwide. Not far from Westminster Cathedral, running
down to Lambeth Bridge, is Horseferry Road, named after the only horse
ferry allowed on the Thames near London and believed to have been even
older than London Bridge, the first bridge built across the Thames in London.
The right to collect tolls for the ferry belonged to the Archbishops of
Canterbury, whose official residence was Lambeth Palace on the south bank

Above:

HMS *Belfast*

The cruiser HMS *Belfast*, a unique and powerful reminder of Britain's naval heritage, was opened as a museum in 1971.

of the Thames beside Lambeth Bridge. Records of building on the site of Lambeth Palace date back to the late 12th century, but between 1828 and 1834 the structure was rebuilt, with the residential part of the palace being completely reconstructed in the Gothic style.

Running north from Parliament Square is Whitehall, in which stands the Cenotaph. Devoid of any religious symbols, this is a national memorial to the "Glorious Dead" of both world wars. Every year, on the Sunday nearest to November 11, a service is held at the Cenotaph to remember those who were killed in action. A gun salute is followed by one minute's silence, after which wreaths are laid. Almost directly opposite the Cenotaph is Downing Street where Number 10 has been the home of British prime ministers since 1732. George II (1683–1760) offered the house to Sir Robert Walpole (1676–1745) and it has remained the premier's residence since.

The north end of Whitehall runs into Trafalgar Square with its famous column and statue of Lord Nelson (1758–1805). The column reaches 185 feet into the sky, and at its foot lie Landseer's (1802–73) lions. Trafalgar Square was laid out in honor of Lord Nelson to commemorate his last and greatest victory—the battle of Trafalgar in 1805. Admiralty Arch is situated in the south-west corner of Trafalgar Square and separates the Mall from the square. The arch dates back to the turn on the century when the Royal Navy ruled the waves and the Admiralty—navy department—was of great importance. Trafalgar Square has long been the meeting place for political demonstrations and, today, is often the terminal point for marches. For the tourists and locals alike, feeding the pigeons and jumping in the fountains have become traditional pastimes in the square.

East from Trafalgar Square is the Strand, originally a bridle path running alongside the Thames, hence the name. A street with shops, hotels, theaters and restaurants, it is one of the main links between the West End and the City. In the 1890s the Strand contained more theaters than any other street in London, but today only three remain—the Savoy, the Adelphi, and the Vaudeville. North of Trafalgar Square stands Covent Garden, designed by the architect Inigo Jones in the early 17th century. London's first formal square surrounded by town houses, it eventually became an important fruit, flower, and vegetable market until 1974 when the market was moved to its new site in Nine Elms. Complete restoration has since transformed Covent Garden into an attractive area of fine restaurants and specialist shops, and in the summer months a wide variety of street entertainers and musicians perform there. The Royal Opera House, standing in the north-east corner of Covent Garden, has been host to the world's top opera and ballet stars in its renowned lavish productions. Covent Garden served as a model for many of the fashionable "squares" in the neighboring districts of Soho, Mayfair, Belgravia, Bloomsbury, and Marylebone.

In the heart of the West End, cosmopolitan Soho is bounded by Oxford Street, Regent Street, Shaftesbury Avenue, and Charing Cross Road. Soho was London's principal foreign quarter in the late 17th century when thousands of French Protestants were forced to flee France after the Revocation of the Edict of Nantes. The area has largely lost its former sleazy image and many of London's finest restaurants and liveliest nightclubs are located here. Tucked away near Regent Street, Carnaby Street was the focal point of popular London fashion throughout the "swinging sixties" and is still considered a "must" for the modern tourist. Piccadilly Circus lies in the south-west corner of Soho and is known worldwide for its electronic advertising signs and its statue of Eros. The statue sits atop a memorial fountain, erected in the memory of the philanthropic 7th Earl of Shaftesbury (1801–85), and was originally intended to represent the angel of Christian charity, not Eros, the Greek god of love.

South of Piccadilly lie Green Park and St. James's Park, separated by Constitution Hill and the Mall—the ceremonial route to Buckingham Palace. Green Park is said to have been the burial ground for lepers from nearby St. James's Hospital, which is supposedly why there are no flowers in it. It was enclosed by Henry VIII and turned into a royal park by Charles II. St. James's Park, the oldest and one of the smaller of the royal parks, is a beautiful open space that contains wild fowl breeding on the islands in the lake.

St. James's Palace lies on the north side of the Mall as it passes through the park. The original palace was started by Henry VII (1457–1509) in 1531 and was the sovereign's official London residence. Today, foreign ambassadors are still appointed to the Court of St. James's. On the north side of the building the Gatehouse is the main remnant of the Tudor building and has the initials of Henry VIII and Anne Boleyn (c. 1507–36) carved over the doors. Several royal marriages have been solemnized at the palace, including those of William III (1650–1702) and Mary (1662–94), Queen Anne (1665–1714), George IV (1762–1830), Victoria (1819–1901), and George V (1865–1936). Charles II was born there, and in Friary Court the new sovereign is proclaimed from the balcony by the heralds. In Stable Yard, within the confines of the palace, stands Clarence House, designed by Nash (1752–1835) for William IV (1765–1837) when he was Duke of Clarence. The house was restored for Princess Elizabeth (1926–) before her accession as Elizabeth II in 1952, and is now the home of Queen Elizabeth, the Queen Mother (1900–).

Buckingham Palace, the official London residence of the royal family and the most famous royal home in the world, has been the residence of the monarch since 1837 when Queen Victoria moved her court from St. James's Palace just down the road on the Mall. This famous palace, built in 1703, was formerly known as Buckingham House and was owned by the Duke of Buckingham. It was subsequently bought by George III (1738–1820) in 1762 and later the architect Nash altered and remodeled it for George IV in 1825 when its name was changed to Buckingham Palace. It remained fairly unused until Queen Victoria came to the throne in 1837 and moved her court there. The ceremony of the Changing of the Guard is carried out by the Brigade of Guards—at 11:30 am every day in the summer and on alternate days in the winter—in the palace forecourt, and is a popular tourist attraction. The neo-classical facade behind the forecourt only dates from 1913, but the west wing remains largely as Nash designed it. The architect's great gateway, which was to have stood at the end of the Mall, proved too narrow for the State Coach, and the gate was moved in its entirety to the other side of Hyde Park and its present site, Marble Arch.

Hyde Park, which covers an area of over 340 acres, was in fact opened to the public by Charles I (1600–1649) in 1635. It stretches from the Bayswater Road in the north to Knightsbridge in the south, and from Park Lane in the east to where it merges with Kensington Gardens in the west. The boundary between Kensington Gardens and Hyde Park follows a line from Alexander Gate in the south, over Serpentine Bridge, and up Buck Hill Walk to Victoria Gate in the north. Today the park is a popular spot to walk, ride or, weather permitting, sunbathe.

When William III came to live at Kensington Palace at the end of the 17th century he had three hundred lamps hung from the trees along the *route du roi* (road of kings) which is today known as Rotten Row. It was the first road in England to be lit at night and was meant to be a deterrent to highwaymen. The palace, originally a Jacobean mansion, was reconstructed by Wren and

Above:

Buckingham Palace

The neo-classical facade of Buckingham Palace, the official London
residence of the royal family and the most famous royal home
in the world.

Hawksmoor (1661–1736) on the orders of William and Mary, who took great interest in the gardens. Later, Queen Anne who was not fond of the formal Dutch garden, had them uprooted and new plans drawn up. The gardens we see today are more or less as those planned. George II (1683–1760) died at Kensington Palace, Queen Victoria was born there and it was the principal private royal residence until she became queen. It is now the residence of Princess Margaret, and the state apartments are open to the public.

To the south of Kensington Gardens stands the Albert Memorial. This has been refurbished recently at considerable expense. It was designed by Sir Glbert Scott (1811–78), was built as a national memorial to Prince Albert (1819–61), consort to Queen Victoria and was erected 1863–76. Directly across the road from the memorial stands the Albert Hall, originally meant to be the "Hall of Arts and Sciences," but was prefaced with "Royal Albert" by Queen Victoria during the laying of the foundation stone.

Going south from the Albert Hall we come to the boroughs of Kensington and Chelsea, where some of London's best-known museums, including the Natural History Museum, the Geological Musuem, the Science Museum, and the Victoria and Albert Museum, lie within a short walk from each other. Also in the area is the Chelsea Royal Hospital, founded by Charles II in 1682 and famous for its "Chelsea Pensioners" with their distinctive scarlet tunics and three-cornered hats. The hospital was built by the king as a home for veteran soldiers, a purpose it still fulfills today. The nearby King's Road once formed part of Charles II's private carriage route to Hampton Court. This lively and

Above:

Leicester Square

The statue of William Shakespeare in Leicester Square. The Odeon
cinema in the background is just one of the many cinemas that abound
in this area.

exciting thoroughfare has, since the 1960s, been known for its chic fashion
boutiques and trendy nightclubs and restaurants.

To the north, London spreads outwards through areas like Bloomsbury and
Paddington Green and beyond to the old villages of Hampstead and Highgate,
each standing on a steep hill. Today Islington with its Camden Passage, an
alley noted for its antique shops and market, is a very desirable residential
area. To the west of Islington, down the Euston and Marylebone Roads, lies
Marylebone the home of the fictional detective, Sherlock Holmes, the Wallace
Collection in Manchester Square, and the Courtauld Institute of Art in
Portman Square. Marylebone Road is where the tourist attractions Madame
Tussauds and the Planetarium are situated.

Heading north from Marylebone the Regent's Canal wends its way through
Regent's Park. Although its use as a hunting ground dates back to Henry VIII,
Regent's Park as we know it today was created as part of the Prince Regent's
grand design for a neo-classical development, under the brilliant guidance of
the architect John Nash. Cornwall Terrace (c. 1820), which forms part of the
southern boundary of the park, was the first of the Nash terraces built in the
park; part of it now houses the British Academy. In 1827 the northern area of
the park was laid out for the zoo. Throughout the 1960s and 1970s new build-

ings were added, and London Zoo became one of the biggest tourist attractions in the capital, as well as a center for research. In an anti-clockwise direction round the Outer Circle from the zoo stands the magnificent Central London Mosque with its gold roof. The Islamic Cultural Center which includes the Mosque has been established since 1944. The site was presented as an unconditional gift from the British Government to the U.K. Muslim Community in Britain to enable the latter to conduct the affairs pertaining to their faith.

Although Regent's Park suffered severe bomb damage during the Second World War and neglect afterward, there was a great will and determination to restore it to its former glory. By the late 1970s, with the refurbishment of the eastern boundary of the park including Gloucester, Cumberland, and Chester Terraces, the rehabilitation was complete. In the center of the park, within the boundaries of the Inner Circle, lies Queen Mary's Gardens, with the Open Air Theatre at the northern perimeter. From 1839 to 1932 the gardens belonged to the Royal Botanic Society.

To the north of Regent's Park, situated on twin hills, stand the villages of Hampstead and Highgate. Until the 18th century Hampstead was merely an attractive village outside London but, with the discovery of a mineral spring, it rapidly grew in size and population and fashionable society flocked to the village. Many streets in the "village" survive from that time and, together with Hampstead Heath, give the area the special character that it enjoys today. Hampstead Heath, including Parliament Hill, covers 790 acres and is a popular place for Londoners to go to "the country." After the Great Fire of 1666, much of the woodland of the Heath was cleared to provide timber for the rebuilding of London. The area has long been associated with artists and poets such as Constable (1776–1837)—one of his paintings of the Heath hangs in the Tate Gallery—and Keats (1795–1821). In Hampstead village, the "Flask" public house, so named because flasks of Hampstead water were filled there, was often visited by Hogarth (1697–1764) and by Karl Marx (1818–83) who is buried just up the road in Highgate Cemetery.

Two other taverns of note situated in Hampstead are "Jack Straw's Castle," named after one of the leaders of the Peasant's Revolt (1381), and the "Spaniards," said to have been used by Dick Turpin. "Jack Straw's Castle" is an old coaching inn which was patronized by Dickens (1812–70) and Thackeray (1811–63)—it was rebuilt in 1964. In 1780 a party of Gordon Rioters (petitioners against the repeal of the anti-Roman Catholic legislation), on their way to destroy Kenwood House, were invited in for a drink by the landlord of the "Spaniards" and kept there until a detachment of soldiers arrived and disarmed them—their rifles can still be seen at the bar. Highgate village stands on a twin hill to Hampstead, and also retains, almost unchanged, streets from the 18th century. The Grove is a delightful street with houses dating from the late 17th and early 18th century and, near the foot of Highgate

Hill, stands the Whittington Stone where Dick Whittington is supposed to have been resting with his cat when he heard the sound of the Bow Bells calling him back to the city where he was to become the lord mayor.

Heading up the Thames from Westminster in a westward direction we come to Putney, the starting point the Oxford and Cambridge University Boat Race. The four-mile or so course of the race follows the Thames upstream from Putney to Mortlake. Further upstream of Mortlake are the Royal Botanical Gardens at Kew. The gardens, which are a combination of scientific center and tourist attraction, cover an area of 300 acres. The grounds were extensively altered and improved by the famous landscape gardener Capability Brown (1716–83) around 1770. Their present-day success is due to the eminent 19th-century botanist Sir Joseph Banks (1743–1820). In 1841 the Botanic Gardens were presented to the nation by means of a Royal Commission.

To the west of Kew Gardens stands Syon House, a stone-built turreted quadrangle which was home to the Dukes of Northumberland from 1594. It has many historical and royal connections and its lovely gardens were also laid out by Capability Brown. The Great Conservatory at Syon House is home to one of the finest private collections of tropical plants in the country.

After Kew the Thames then continues on past Ham House, a 17th century mansion, and the wide-open spaces of Richmond Park and its 2,400 acres of open land, herds of deer, and rhododendrons. Eventually, at Teddington, the Thames ceases to be tidal and a system of locks come into operation. The largest tourist attraction to the west of London has to be Hampton Court Palace. The site was bought in 1514 by Cardinal Wolsey (c. 1475–1530) who later presented the building to Henry VIII in a futile attempt to stave off his downfall. Henry was very fond of Hampton Court, and he moved in with his new love of the time, Anne Boleyn, though they were not yet married. He used to travel up the Thames from london to Hampton Court in ceremonial barges and disembark at a water-gate where an elaborate summer house was built; it still stands today. Five of Henry VIII's wives lived at Hampton Court, and the ghosts of two of them are said to haunt the palace still. Elizabeth I added extensively to the gardens of the palace with plants brought from the New World by Hawkins (1532–95), Raleigh, and Drake (c. 1541–96). When Charles II was restored to the throne he was determined to imitate the grandeur of Versailles, which he had seen during his exile in France. During his reign — and that of William and Mary — extensive gardens were laid out in much the same form as they are today. The famous maze was created by William after the death of Mary. The last monarch to live at Hampton Court was George II, after which it became a series of "grace and favor" residences. Upstream from old royal palace the Thames meanders tranquilly through the Surrey and Berkshire meadows to Windsor Castle and Oxford.

Apart from its many fashionable shops located in areas such as the West End, Chelsea, and Kensington, London also boasts several renowned markets,

Above:
Leicester Square

As with so many locations favoured by tourists, Leicester Square has gained a ragtag collection of artists many of whose charges are greater than their talents.

Covent Garden for vegetables and flowers, Billingsgate for fish, and Smithfield for meat. Smithfield meat market was known in the Middle Ages for its horse market; the existing structure was opened in 1868, designed by Sir Horace Jones (1819–87) and modeled on Paxton's Crystal Palace. Smithfield was originally a field where animals were penned for selling but it grew to become the world's largest meat market. The central hall, built in 1866, could handle 400 truckloads of meat at any one time. As mentioned earlier, London's original, premier vegetable market moved from the Covent Garden area just off the Strand, to Nine Elms in Battersea but the old market halls have been preserved and now house shops, boutiques, and restaurants. The original Billingsgate fish market developed around a "river gate" in the city wall where a harbor was built. By the 17th century the bad language of fish porters and fishwives made Billingsgate and swearing synonymous. The market moved further downriver to the Isle of Dogs in 1982.

Along with the large produce markets London boasts several famous street markets. Petticoat Lane market is actually situated in Middlesex Street. It grew originally as a market for second-hand clothes, where the local poor could buy the cast-offs of the rich, but today the market attracts hundreds of tourists looking for bric-a-brac, and more upmarket antiques on Fridays and Saturdays. Camden Lock, on the Regent's Canal, boasts a very colorful and exotic market, with a profusion of ethnic restaurants and lively bars in the surrounding area. Lambeth Walk, south of Lambeth Palace, hosts a busy general

Above:

Interior of the Royal Opera House

Opened in 1732, the first theater on the site was said to be the most luxurious ever created; it and its successor burned down. Today's building—recently having undergone major refurbishment—was designed by E.M. Barry in 1858.

street market open seven days a week. This market grew up in the 19th century and was well-established by the 1840s. Other street markets include, Portobello Road in Kensington, open every Friday and Saturday, Camden Passage in Islington, which has antique stalls, Leather Lane off Holborn, which sells a variety of bric-a-brac, and further out, Brixton and Kingston represent good examples of the 100 or so London street markets.

Markets are part of London's cultural past but museums and art galleries reflect the past in a different way, and the city has an abundance of these. Situated in Trafalgar Square, the National Gallery houses the national collection of Western European paintings. The paintings date from the 13th century to the 20th century and virtually the entire collection is displayed. Nearby, the National Portrait Gallery houses nearly ten thousand portraits of the people who shaped the British nation and is the most extensive collection of its kind in the world. In addition to paintings the collection includes sculptures, miniatures, engravings, and photographs. On the Embankment the Tate Gallery, opened in 1897, is home to the national collections of British art and international modern art. The works in the Tate trace the development of art from the Impressionists to post-war European and American art. It is especially renowned for its modern works of art, some of which have aroused great controversy. In the City, the Barbican, named after an outer fortification of the old city, houses the Museum of London and the Barbican Center of Arts and

Conferences. Officially opened by the Queen in 1982, this includes an art gallery, three cinemas, a concert hall, and a 1,166-seat theater.

Out of town, Dulwich Picture Gallery is a gallery based in picturesque Dulwich Village to the south of the City. The gallery is one of the hidden gems of Southwark containing an outstanding collection of Old Masters, mainly from the 17th and 18th centuries. Dulwich College decided to build an art gallery, and Sir John Soane (1753–1837) was commissioned to design one of the first purpose-built picture galleries in Britain. The buildings were completed in 1813, at a cost of £9,778. The collection has been further built up and now contains works by the likes of Rembrandt (1606–69), Van Dyck (1599–1641), Rubens (1577–1640), and Canaletto (1697–1768). To the north, on Hampstead Heath, Kenwood House is home to the Iveagh Bequest which includes works by Van Dyck, Gainsborough (1727–88), Reynolds (1723–92), Rembrandt, Landseer (1802–73), and Turner (1775–1851). Kenwood House was purchased in 1754 by the 1st Earl of Mansfield and transformed for him by Robert Adam (1728–92) into the magnificent mansion that stands today. It was bought by Edward Cecil Guinness, 1st Earl of Iveagh, (1847–1927) in 1924 and is open to the public.

London also is home to some of the world's most famous museums. The British Museum, founded in 1753, contains world-famous collections of antiquities from Egypt, Western Asia, Greece, and Rome as well as Prehistoric and Romano-British artifacts. It also boasts collections of Medieval, Renaissance, Modern, and Oriental collections, prints and drawings, coins, banknotes, and medals. The old Royal Library, which had been founded by Henry VII, was presented to the trustees of the museum by George II and incorporated into the museum in 1757. With this library came the privilege of compulsory copyright, which means that a copy of every book published in the country has to be presented free to the museum.

South of the River Thames, to the east of Lambeth Palace, the Imperial War Museum uniquely covers the history of world conflict from World War I to the present day. The museum is fortunate to have a wide range of exhibits including tanks, guns, and aircraft. It also includes a walk through recreation of a front-line trench at the Somme in 1916 and a blitzed London street from 1940. There is also a gallery dedicated to the world of secret warfare, from 1914 to the present day. The museum deals with all aspects of war, from the military hero to the conscientious objector, the home front and the front line. It recognizes that war is a serious subject worthy of study, but does not glorify conflict. We are reminded of the millions who have perished as a result of war this century. The building which houses the museum was previously the Bethlehem Royal Hospital—the original Bedlam.

People interested in the history of warfare may like to visit HMS *Belfast*, moored permanently as a museum on the River Thames in the Pool of London, and a unique and powerful reminder of Britain's naval heritage. *Belfast* was a cruiser launched in 1938 and served with distinction in both the Second World War and the Korean War and is now the only surviving example of the great fleets of big gun armored warships built for the Royal Navy in the first half of the 20th century. She was opened as a museum in 1971 and is the first ship to be preserved for the nation since Nelson's flagship HMS *Victory*.

In west London, in Kensington, the collection of museums that stand on or near Exhibition Road owe their existence to the energy and enthusiasm of Prince Albert. It was his tireless persistence that resulted in the Great Exhibition being opened in Hyde Park in 1851. Its unqualified success persuaded Albert that the profits made from it should be used to purchase land on which would be built an array of educational establishments. In 1856, the Gore Estate, on which the museums now stand, was purchased and building work, which continues to the present day, began.

The Victoria and Albert Museum is the largest museum of the decorative arts in the world. It was founded in 1852 as the South Kensington Museum, and in 1899 it was renamed the Victoria and Albert Museum in honor of Queen Victoria and Prince Albert. The laying of the foundation stone of the museum was the last important public engagement by Queen Victoria. It was not, however, until 1909 that this imposing terracotta brick building was officially opened by Edward VII (1841–1910). Today the beautiful Victorian and Edwardian buildings house 145 galleries containing some of the world's greatest collections of sculpture, furniture, fashion, and textiles, paintings, silver, glass, ceramics, jewelry, books, prints, and photographs.

Also situated in Kensington, the Natural History Museum is dedicated to furthering the understanding of the natural world through its unrivaled collections, its world class exhibitions, and through its internationally significant program of scientific research. The life and earth science collections of the museum comprise some 68 million specimens or items that cover virtually all groups of animals, plants, minerals, and fossils. The science departments include botany, entomology, mineralogy, palaeontology, and zoology. The museum was opened in 1881 to exhibit the ever expanding collections which were originally housed in the British Museum. The museum is housed in a vast and elaborate Romanesque-style building faced with terracotta slabs bearing animal, birds, and fishes molded in relief.

The collections in the Science Musuem cover the application of science to technology and the development of engineering and industry from their early beginnings to the present day. The museum is housed in an impressive building that was completed in 1928 and added to in the 1960s. The collections, which now include the *Apollo 10* space capsule, *Puffing Billy*—the world's first locomotive, and George Stephenson's *Rocket*, originally formed part of the old South Kensington Museum. The Geological Museum is the national museum of earth sciences. It illustrates the general principles of geological science together with earth history and the regional geology of Britain. The museum

Above:

Tower Bridge

One of the most distinctive of London's landmarks, the bridge was designed by city architect Sir Horace Jones and opened in 1894. Its two stone-clad towers hide steel frames and lifts originally designed to take pedestrians to two high-level walkways.

was established in 1837 as a direct result of the Geological Survey of Great Britain and the exhibits, which include a stunningly beautiful collection of gem stones, were moved to their present location in 1935—the centenary of the Geological Survey.

Along with its "mainstream" museums London has some delightfully unusual exhibitions. The Bramah Tea and Coffee Museum allows the visitor to explore the history and traditions of these two important beverages amongst the tea warehouses of Butlers Wharf. From the 17th century coffee houses to the coffee bars of the 1950s and from Oriental traditions to the teabag you can find out everything you ever wanted to know about tea and coffee. At its peak Butlers Wharf used to handle 6,000 chests of tea a day.

To the north of the City the London Canal Museum tells the story of the canals, the people who lived and worked on them, the cargoes they carried, and the horses which towed the boats. The museum is housed in a former ice warehouse built in about 1862–63 for Carlo Gatti, the famous ice cream maker, and features the history of the ice trade and ice cream as well as the canals. This is the only London museum of inland waterways and is situated at King's Cross, an accessible central London location.

Above:
St Paul's Cathedral
Sir Christopher Wren's masterpiece, St. Paul's Cathedral is one of
London's most famous landmarks. It was designed and constructed
after the Great Fire of London.

Out to the west, the Kew Bridge Steam Museum houses a collection of steam pumping engines including the largest running and largest existing single cylinder engines in the world. The museum also has its own narrow gauge railway and is currently developing a display of the history of water supply. The museum is housed in a magnificent 19th century pumping station and centers around the station's five world famous Cornish beam engines. Originally used to pump West London's water supply for more than a century, one of them, the *Grand Junction 90* is the world's biggest working beam engine. Many Victorian waterworks had their own railway and at Kew bridge this is demonstrated by a short line featuring the steam locomotive *Cloister*.

Deep in the heart of London, buried beneath London Bridge Station, the London Dungeon, billed as a museum with a difference, is a unique museum of 40 spine-chilling exhibits and is now one of the capital's top tourist attractions. Within the Dungeon you can step back in time and journey through the darker side of European history. The museum features a wide variety of attractions including modern multimedia displays, actors, and special effects.

For those with a less morbid taste the Museum of the Moving Image (MOMI) is an interactive museum where the visitor gets to be the star of the show! The world of film and television comes to life as you get to fly like Superman, audition for a part in a Hollywood film, and interact with a cast of actors—it's brilliant for children of all ages, as is the London Transport Museum in Covent Garden, noted for its old red buses and historic tube trains.

The renowned theaters of London attract tourists from all over the world and it is not just the glitzy shows of the West End's "theaterland" that fascinate these theater lovers. Attending a performance at the newly opened Globe Theatre is a truly unique experience taking you back to the age of Tudor theater. The Globe Theatre is the sixth biggest auditorium in London with seating for 1,000 and 500 standing. To maintain authenticity there is no roof and no lighting meaning that performances can only take place during daylight in the more favorable seasons. Near Waterloo Station the National Theatre, with its three theaters—the Cottesloe, the Lyttleton, and the Olivier—forms part of the "South Bank" arts complex. The complex also includes the Royal Festival Hall, the Queen Elizabeth Hall, the National Film Theatre and MOMI.

Last but not least, London is a paradise for the epicure, with its pubs and restaurants catering for every conceivable taste. There are over 7,000 pubs in London ranging in appearance from labyrinthine coaching inns to basic bars on humble street corners. It must be remembered, however, that many of the City pubs are not open at weekends and out of business hours. The range of restaurants equals that of the pubs and concentrated in the West End alone are several hundred restaurants catering for most tastes and pockets. Most nationalities with a reputation for cuisine are represented somewhere in central London.

Getting to visit all the tourist attractions in London is made easy by the capital's famous red buses, black taxis, and the London Underground—"the tube." The first "tube" railway in the world opened in 1870 and was a cable-operated car which ran through a subway between Tower Hill and Bermondsey. From this small beginning the nine lines and 275 stations of the present system now make up one of the largest electric underground railways in the world. The Underground is the quickest and most efficient way to get around the capital and there is almost always an Underground station close at hand throughout London.

Following on from the Parisian precedent a regular omnibus service was first seen in London in 1829. The first horse drawn omnibuses seated 22 passengers and they were finally withdrawn in 1916 after the first gas-driven bus was introduced in 1910. The large tram network of the late 19th and early 20th centuries was succeeded by trolley-buses, then eventually gas-driven buses gave way to today's diesel-engine vehicles. The indomitable London red bus is not only one of the most famous in the world but also one of the safest, having to undergo very rigorous safety tests.

Like the New York yellow cabs, the black London taxi, with its distinctive shape, is instantly recognizable. Taxis are a salvation for those who get lost and are a godsend in the early hours when the main transport systems have shut down. London cabbies are very experienced and know their way about—they have to undergo "The Knowledge," a test to make sure they know London inside out, before they can obtain their licence. Taxis can be called by telephone but they can also be "hailed" in the street if they are displaying their illuminated "For Hire" sign.

Another way to travel in London is by water transport. The Thames perhaps isn't exploited in this way as much as it should be but a very pleasant stretch of water is the Regent's Canal which was opened in 1820. Starting from Little Venice, which forms the junction of the Paddington arm of the Grand Union Canal and the Regent's Canal, it runs into Limehouse Basin. Passing through Regent's Park, the stretch between Little Venice and Camden Town follows the Outer Circle round the park's northern and western perimeters and is always busy with leisure traffic in the summer. Pleasure boat trips are available from the Zoological Gardens to Little Venice.

Today, at the beginning of a new millennium, tourists are attracted to London for many reasons including the historical heritage of the city and the modern West End—the shopping center of Britain—as well as the vibrant nightlife with many restaurants, night clubs, cinemas, hotels, and "theaterland." Modern London is a cosmopolitan, multi-racial city with a large immigrant population from Britain's former colonies, especially from South Asia and the West Indies. Some quarters of the city are dominated by specific ethnic groups and visitors can enjoy the culture and unique cuisines from their original homelands. London attracts millions of visitors each year, and tourism, especially in the summer, is a major industry and contributor to the economy. Intercontinental and European visitors to London are ably served by Heathrow Airport to the west and Gatwick Airport to the south. The smaller airports of Luton and Standsted are also quite capable of handling these flights and with the opening of the Channel Tunnel visitors from Continental Europe can reach the center of London with remarkable ease.

Right:
Albert Memorial
The Albert Memorial, erected 1863–76 and recently refurbished, was built as a national memorial to Prince Albert, Consort to Queen Victoria.

PALM COU

Ice Rink

Above:
Battersea Power Station
The bold, uncompromising appearance of Battersea Power Station caused quite a sensation when it was completed in the early 1950s. Today it is a listed building.

Right:
Bank of England
The magnificent neo-classical building of the "Old Lady of Threadneedle Street"—the Bank of England. The vaults of the Bank traditionally house the nation's gold reserves.

Previous page:
Alexandra Palace
North London's answer to the Crystal Palace opened in 1873 and suffered a similar fate to its rival in 1980, when much succumbed to fire. It was the world's first television transmitting station in 1936.

Above:
Buckingham Palace
A view of Buckingham Palace from across the lake in St. James's Park. The palace was bought by George III,
rebuilt by George IV, and enlarged by Queen Victoria.

Right:
Queen Victoria Monument
The gilded monument to Queen Victoria, the first monarch to hold court at Buckingham Palace,
stands outside the front gates of the palace.

Above:
Camden Lock
The area surrounding Camden Lock boasts a very colorful and exotic market,
with a profusion of ethnic restaurants and lively bars.

Right:
Canary Wharf
This imposing tower, standing at 800 feet, with its shining, pyramidal top can be seen from
the most unexpected places throughout London.

Above:

Carnaby Street

Built in the 18th century for "poor and miserable objects of the neighborhood," Carnaby Street became the focal
point of popular London fashion throughout the "swinging sixties."

Right:

The City

A view of a busy street in the City, the center of commerce in London, with the indomitable
London red double-decker bus in the foreground.

Above:
Covent Garden
In the summer months a wide variety of street entertainers and musicians perform here
in the plaza of the refurbished Covent Garden.

Right:
Covent Garden
When the old Covent Garden fruit and vegetable market moved complete restoration transformed the area into
an attractive area of fine restaurants and specialist shops.

Previous page:
Chinatown
Between Soho and Leicester Square, concentrating on Gerrard Street, is London's Chinatown. Always bustling
with restaurants and shops, it bursts into life at the Chinese New Year with dragons and fireworks.

Above:

Cutty Sark

The *Cutty Sark*, the last and most famous of the old tea clippers,
was brought to dry dock in Greenwich in 1954.

Right:

"Dickens" Inn, St. Katherine's Dock

St. Katherine's Dock, a complex of superb warehouses (the inn was adapted from one such) and basins, was
closed in 1968. Since then the buildings have been restored and adapted for a variety of uses.

Above:

10 Downing Street

Ten Downing Street, the home of British prime ministers ever since 1732,
when George II offered the house to Sir Robert Walpole.

Right:

The Cenotaph

The Cenotaph is a national war memorial where every year a service is held
to remember the "Glorious Dead" of both world wars.

Above:

Globe Theatre

The newly opened Globe Theatre where attending a performance is a truly unique experience taking you back to the age of Tudor theater.

Right:

Green Park

Green Park, said to have originally been the burial ground for lepers, was enclosed by Henry VIII and turned into a royal park by Charles II.

Above:
Hampstead Heath
Hampstead Heath is a popular place for Londoners to go to "the country,"
and has long been associated with renowned artists and poets.

Right:
Guildhall
The Great Hall of the Guildhall is used for the Lord Mayor's Banquet
and is decorated with the colorful shields of the livery companies.

Above and Previous page:
Imperial War Museum

The Imperial War Museum covers the history of world conflict from World War I to
the present day. The inhabitants of the row of houses opposite had to be reassured that the naval guns at the
entrance, if fired (they are, of course, decommissioned), would not hit them. The people of Watford
may have been less reassured by the answer!

Right:
Kensington Gardens

The statue of Edward Jenner (1749–1823), pioneer of vaccination, in the gardens of Kensington Palace.
The gardens are more or less unchanged since Queen Anne's days.

Above:

Lambeth Palace

The Tudor brickwork of Morton's Tower, the main entrance to Lambeth Palace, is one of London's
few surviving medieval buildings.

Right:

Law Courts

The Royal Courts of Justice, generally called the Law Courts, were designed in the Gothic style
by the distinguished Victorian architect George Edmund Street (1824–81).

Above:

Leicester Square

Leicester Square was originally laid out in Victorian times as a garden and takes its name from Leicester House,
a large mansion which once stood on the site.

Right:

Charlie Chaplin at Leicester Square

The statue of Charlie Chaplin (1889–1977) in Leicester Square is just one of the monuments
to famous people situated here.

Previous page:

Lambeth Palace

The Archbishop of Canterbury's official residence in London, it dates back to the 12th century
although extensively rebuilt in 1828–34.

Above:

Life Guards — the Household Cavalry

Seven regiments of guards defend the sovereign: five of foot (Grenadier, Coldstream, Scots, Irish, and Welsh)
and two of horse (the Life Guards — one pictured here — and the Blues and Royals).

Right:

"Lincoln" Inn, Marylebone

There are over 7,000 pubs in London catering for every conceivable taste, this mock Tudor building houses a
typical London West End hostelry.

Above:
Lloyd's Building
This edifice, designed by the architect Richard Rogers (1933–), is the latest in a series of buildings to house
Lloyd's, the world's premier insurance market.

Right:
London Eye Ferris Wheel
The London Eye, the biggest ferris wheel in the world, was the centerpiece of London's millennium celebrations.
The 324-ton structure holds 32 rotating pods.

Previous page:
London Dungeon
Tooley Street is home to an interesting, if occasionally macabre, recreation
of some of the more bloody moments of English history.

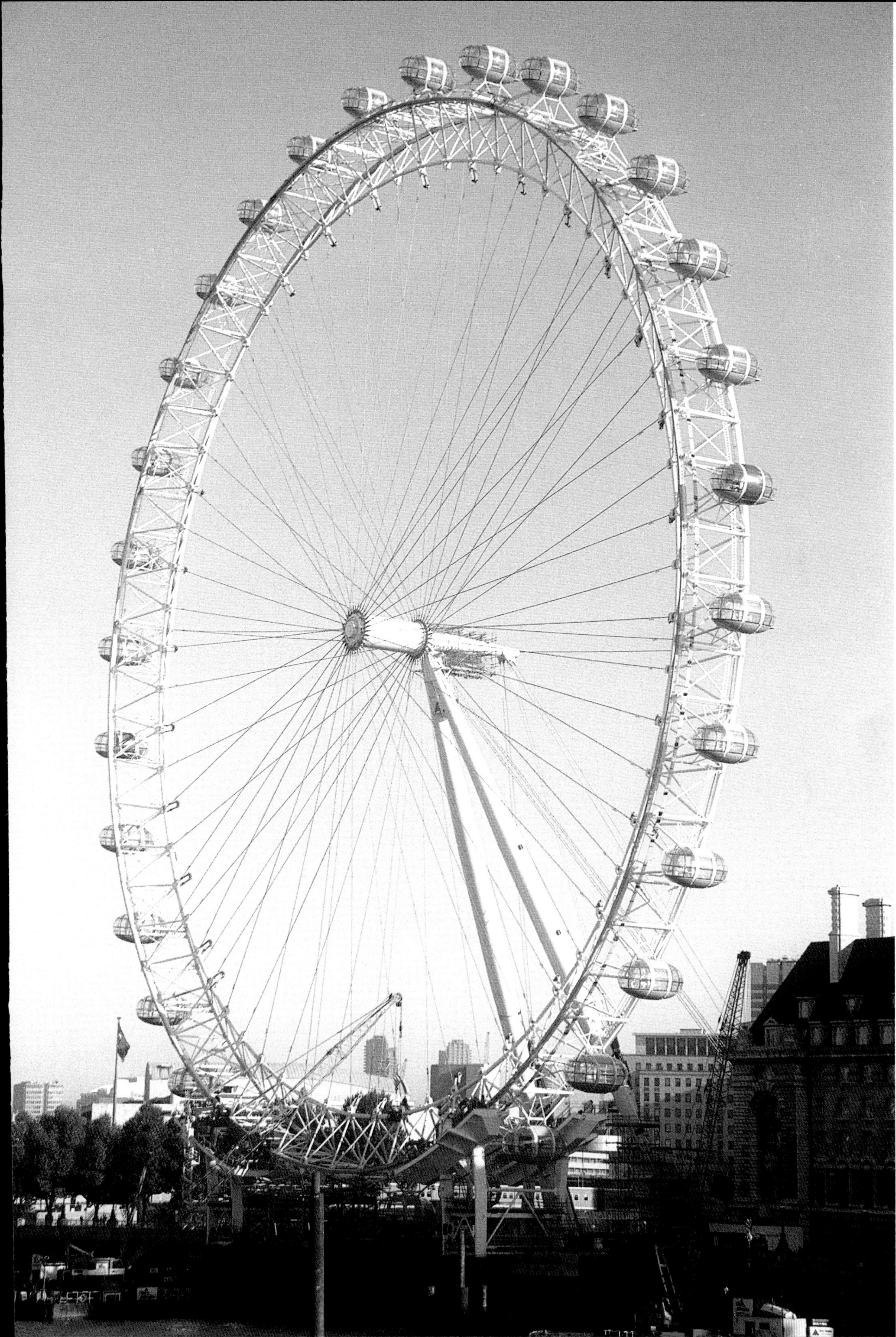

Above:

Madame Tussaud's & the Planetarium

Madame Tussauds stands adjacent to the Planetarium on the Marylebone Road. Spectacular representations
of the heavens are projected on the inside of the Planetarium's great copper dome.

Right:

The Mall

The Mall passes through St. James's Park and is the ceremonial route to Buckingham Palace
used by visiting royalty and heads of state.

Above:
Marble Arch
Marble Arch, Nash's great gateway originally intended to be the entrance to Buckingham Palace,
was moved in its entirety to its current site.

Right:
The Monument
The Monument (202 feet high) was erected in 1671–77 to commemorate the Great Fire of London
which devastated the City in 1666.

Above:

Natural History Museum

The imposing entrance to the Natural History Museum, which is housed in a vast and elaborate Romanesque-
style building faced with terracotta slabs bearing animals moulded in relief.

Right:

Selfridges

Selfridges is situated on the busy stretch of Oxford Street between Marble Arch and Oxford Circus.

Previous page:

Queen's House, Greenwich

Foreshortened by the telephoto lens, this view of Greenwich from the river looks through
the Royal Naval College, over the Queen's House (commissioned by James I for Anne of Denmark),
to the Royal Observatory atop Greenwich Hill.

Above:
Palladium
The London Palladium is arguably London's best loved variety theater.
Its famous "Sunday Night" live shows used to be televised weekly.

Right:
Picadilly Circus
Piccadilly Circus is known worldwide for its electronic advertising hoardings
and, in the foreground, the statue of Eros.

Previous page:
The Oval
Now the "Foster's Oval" thanks to sponsorship, the Kennington home of Surrey Cricket Club
is one of the most famous cricket grounds in the world.

Above:

Queen Elizabeth Gate—Hyde Park

Hyde Park, which covers an area of over 340 acres, was opened to the public by Charles I in 1635 and is a popular spot to walk, ride, or weather permitting, take an outdoor lunch.

Right:

Regent Street

Regent Street, one of the finest shopping streets in the world, was laid out by the great architect John Nash on the orders of George IV.

Previous page:

Petticoat Lane

One of the largest Victorian street markets, attempts were made in the first half of the 20th century to thwart its Sunday morning opening: luckily, they failed and the market thrives.

Above:
Royal Academy
The Royal Academy was founded by George III and moved to its present site, Burlington House in Picadilly, in 1869. The famous Summer Exhibition is held here every May to August.

Right:
Royal Albert Hall
Named after Queen Victoria's beloved Albert, the huge circular building with its glass dome was originally intended to be the "Hall of Arts and Sciences."

Previous page:
Royal Hospital
Founded by King Charles II in 1682 to care for soldiers who had been wounded in battle as well as those that had retired and could no longer care for themselves. Today it continues to provide a home for the famous Chelsea pensioners.

Above:
Royal Exchange
The Royal Exchange was originally opened in 1568 as a meeting place for City merchants.
Queen Victoria opened the present building in 1844.

Right:
The Royal Courts of Justice
The main entrance to the Royal Courts of Justice has archways flanked by twin towers
through which are the stairways to the public galleries.

Previous page:
Royal Albert Bridge
Constructed 1871–73 to the design of Roland Ordish, the Albert Bridge is a beautiful example
of the technology of Victorian England.

Above:
"Sherlock Holmes" Public House

The "Sherlock Holmes," is another typical London Pub popular with both tourists and local workers.

Right:
The Savoy

In 1884, D'Oyly Carte, who had already built the Savoy Theatre as a home for Gilbert and Sullivans operas, decided to build a hotel to compete with the best in America.

Previous page:
South Bank

Developed post-World War II, the Surrey bank of the Thames boasts the Royal Festival Hall, the Queen Elizabeth Hall, the National Theatre, the Hayward Gallery, and the National Film Theatre: it's just a shame they were all built of concrete.

Above:

St. Pancras

With its high pinnacles, towers and gables, the amazing facade of St. Pancras station looks more like
a Gothic castle than a railway station.

Right:

St. Bartholomew's

The half-timbered Elizabethan gatehouse marking the entrance to the Norman church of
St. Barthlomew the Great, the oldest church standing in the City.

Above:

Dome of St. Paul's

The beautiful, great central dome of St. Paul's Cathedral posed Wren considerable structural problems
but is today one of London's most recognizable landmarks.

Right:

St. Paul's Cathedral

Despite its vulnerability, St. Paul's remained remarkably unscathed during the Luftwaffe's fierce
incediary bomb attacks in the vicinity during World War II.

Above:
Tate Gallery
On the Embankment the Tate Gallery, opened in 1897, is home to the national collections of British
and international modern art.

Right:
"Taxi!"
The black London taxi, with its distinctive shape, is instantly recognizable. This one is plying its trade in
Oxford Street—Selfridges can be seen in the background.

Above:
Tower Bridge
The approaches to Tower Bridge couldn't be built too steeply as Victorian horse drawn carriages had to cross
so a raising bridge was designed.

Right:
Tower Bridge
A famous and distinctive Victorian structure, Tower Bridge is one of the most instantly recognizable bridges in
the world and has become a symbol of London.

Previous page:
Tower of London — The Crown Jewels
Most of the Crown Jewels date from the Restoration of Charles II in 1660, although some earlier pieces
are also on show at the Tower.

Above:
Trafalgar Square
The fountains of Trafalgar Square, which was laid out in honor of Lord Nelson to commemorate his greatest victory over the French, were added in 1948.

Right:
Trafalgar Square
Nelson's Column in Trafalgar Square, a memorial to the nation's greatest sailor, was set up between 1842 and 1867 and stands to a height of almost 185ft.

Previous page:
Twickenham
Headquarters of the Rugby Football Union and home of English rugby,
Twickenham Rugby Football Ground has recently undergone a dramatic renovation.
It's a far cry from "Billy William's Cabbage Patch," bought in 1907 for around £5,500.

Above:

Nelson on his column

The statue of Lord Nelson, standing on top of its famous column, was sculpted by E. H. Bailey and, at 17ft 4in,
is almost the size of an upturned London bus.

Right:

Victoria & Albert Museum

The laying of the foundation stone of this imposing terracotta brick building, which houses the Victoria and
Albert Museum, was the last important public engagement by Queen Victoria.

Above:

West End — Centre Point

Richard Seifert's rhythmic building of the 1960s, generally underrated and the subject of much abuse, dominates the skyline of the West End.

Right:

Westminster — Big Ben

The minute hands on the clock faces of what is popularly known as Big Ben are each as tall as a double-decker bus.

Above:

Westminster — Clock Tower

The famous Clock Tower of the Houses of Parliament known to all as Big Ben.
Big Ben is actually the mighty 13½ ton bell which strikes the hours.

Right:

Westminster Bridge & Palace of Westminster

A view of the Houses of Parliament and the 19th century Westminster Bridge
from the south bank of the Thames.

Above:
Westminster Abbey
Westminster Abbey, the coronation site of English kings and queens since Harold was crowned here in 1065. The Abbey has also long been the setting of royal weddings and somber state occasions.

Right:
Westminster Abbey
Westminster Abbey is a splendid example of English Gothic architecture and was rebuilt by Henry III in 1245, then altered and added to through the succeeding centuries.

INDEX